THE POWER OF THOUGHT CHILDREN'S BOOK SERIES

I HAVE CHOICES

Written by Amber Raymond & Lynn McLaughlin

Illustrated by Allysa Batin

D1716402

We all feel many emotions. The characters in this book glow in the following colours to match how they are feeling.

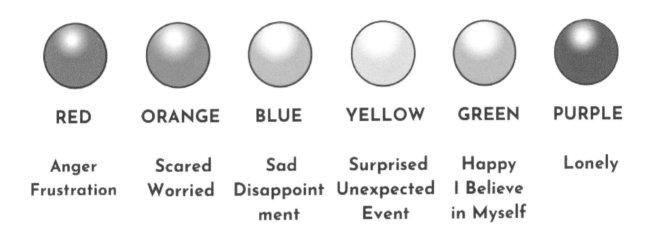

RED	ORANGE	BLUE	YELLOW	GREEN	PURPLE
Anger	Scared	Sad	Surprised	Happy	Lonely
Frustration	Worried	Disappoint ment	Unexpected Event	I Believe in Myself	

- Can you see when each character's feelings are changing?
- Can you tell by the look on their faces, by body language or the words they are using? Maybe you can tell by the colour of their glow.
- Have you ever felt the same way? How do you express your own feelings?

"I can't wait to hang out and play with Nyx today."

"Oh no. Why are they all playing Turbo? I thought it was just me and Nyx hanging out."

"You're glowing very brightly today Zirco," said Trine.
"Are you OK? You look a little worried."

"I'm scared no one will want me on their team.
What if I crash into someone? What if they all
laugh at me?"

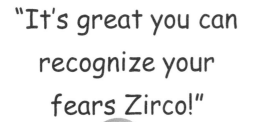

"It's great you can recognize your fears Zirco!"

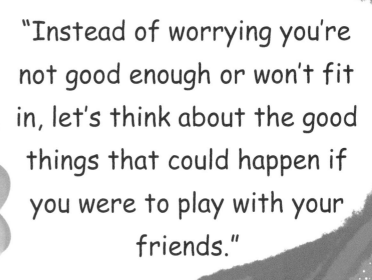

"Instead of worrying you're not good enough or won't fit in, let's think about the good things that could happen if you were to play with your friends."

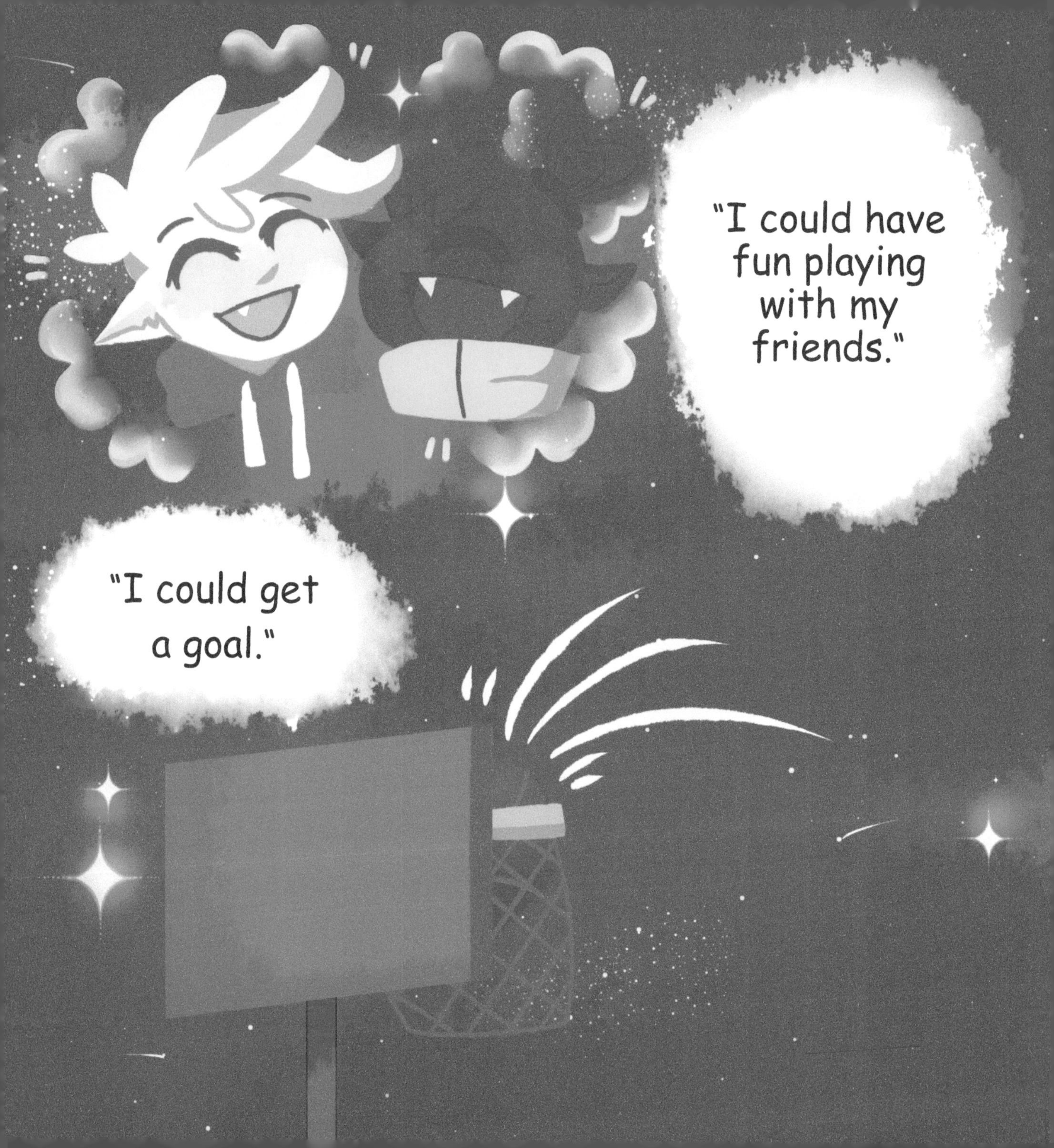
"I could have fun playing with my friends."
"I could get a goal."

"Good job noticing that joining the game could be fun. It seems like thinking good thoughts has helped you to feel less scared."

"I think so too!"

"Sometimes when we're scared it's hard to think clearly and see the good things that can happen. It's helpful to remember we always have a choice. If you decided not to join Nyx playing Turbo, what else could you do?" Trine asked.

"I could play Shuffle with Carnuli so they wont be lonely."
"I could cheer on my friends."

"It sounds like all of your choices will make you happy, I'm not sure how you can go wrong. Aren't you proud of yourself for taking control of your thoughts and fears?"

"Thanks Trine! I am proud of myself!"

"When we have strong emotions, it can be hard to think clearly and see all of the good choices we have. Sometimes our scary thoughts can keep us from enjoying things we love to do."

You Can Do it Too!

1. By reviewing our choices, we can turn our scary thoughts into happy ones.

2. When you can see all the good choices, it's easier to decide what to do.

3. Remember to think about what makes you happy.

4. Make a choice and do it!

Vocabulary

Scared – A feeling that things will happen that you don't want to happen

Happy – A feeling that makes you smile

Positive – Thinking good thoughts

Negative – Thinking sad and unhelpful thoughts

Lonely – A feeling of not wanting to spend time alone (Although being alone can sometimes feel good, there are times when you may want to be with other people).

Like You, Every Crystal is Unique!

Did you notice the characters are all named after crystals?

Some crystals look like simple rocks, and others look like they're from another planet. No matter their appearance, they all make you feel a sense of wonder when you see the way they shine.

Also known as rocks, gemstones, and minerals, crystals are formed through geological processes by heat and pressure underground. Working with crystals can help you transform into the most powerful version of yourself by guiding you to see how

Carnelian (*Carnuli*): empowerment, focus, action and confidence

Citrine (*Trine*): empowerment, confidence, creativity, manifestation and abundance

Lapis Lazuli (*Lazu*): intuition, education, communication and problem solving

Sardonyx (*Nyx*): empowerment, Confidence, leadership, courage, growth and boundaries,

Zircon (*Zirco*): confidence, wisdom, love and happiness

Amber Raymond

BA, BSW, MSW, RSW

WWW.MESSSMAKERS.COM

As a Masters-level Social Worker, Amber is an advocate for non-conventional, evidence-based coping strategies and is devoted to her friends and family.

She is passionate about child mental health, lifelong self-care practices, self-exploration, self-love, and holistic wellbeing.

When not practicing social work, Amber likes to research effective methods for her son and loved ones to overcome life's mental and emotional challenges.

Lynn McLaughlin

MED, BED, BA

WWW.LYNNMCLAUGHLIN.COM

Lynn McLaughlin served as a Superintendent of Education, Administrator and Teacher. Lynn continues to be active in education, teaching future Educational Assistants at her local College.

Lynn hosts the inspirational podcast "Taking the Helm" and publishes a new episode on Wednesdays.

As a best-selling, award-winning author, and Rotarian, Lynn is dedicated to community causes. She is a member of 100 Women Who Care Windsor/Essex and works tirelessly to support the goals of the Brain Tumour Foundation of Canada.

Allysa Batin

:camera: @bats.illustration

Allysa Batin is a young freelance illustrator. She enjoys creating fun and colourful characters and advcating for love and acceptance in her art. Her favourite pastimes include hosting Dungeons & Dragons and taking pictures of her dog.

Watch for other books in *The Power of Thought Series*

Is What I'm Thinking True?
I Can Find My Calm Place
I Can Listen to My Body

 Lightning Source UK Ltd.
Milton Keynes UK
UKHW050630080522
402632UK00002B/68